GOD
any time any place

GOD

any any
time place

The many ways
college students pray

Pegge Bernecker

ave maria press AMP Notre Dame, Indiana

www.avemariapress.com

Founded in 1865, Ave Maria Press is a ministry of the Indiana Province of Holy Cross.

ISBN-10 1-59471-019-8   ISBN-13 978-1-59471-019-3

Cover and text design by John Carson

Cover photo © Corbis / Punchstock

Printed and bound in the United States of America.

Library of Congress Cataloging-in-Publication Data
Bernecker, Pegge.
  God-- any time, any place : the many ways college students pray / Pegge Bernecker.
    p. cm.
  Includes bibliographical references.
  ISBN 1-59471-019-8 (pbk.)
  1. Catholic college students--Religious life. 2. Prayer--Catholic Church.
I. Title.

BX2373.S8B37 2005
248.3'2'088378198--dc22
                              2004024182

To the readers of this little book:

When you glimpse the Holy One sparking brightly in these pages, may you be as inspired and hope-filled as I am.

—PEGGE BERNECKER

Contents

Acknowledgments 9

Introduction 11

Time Made Holy 17

Conversation with God. 31

Gratitude. 43

Catholic Traditions 57

Engaging Bodily Presence 71

Love One Another. 83

Words: Written, Read, Sung 97

Dawn and Dusk. 109

Notes. 123

Acknowledgments

So many people helped shape this book.

In particular the college students that graciously offered their prayer practices, connecting in a virtual world at all hours of the day and night. I am utterly grateful for the glimpse of God I am privileged to witness through your sharing and for the hope you bring to our world. And, for the thousands of students I have met face-to-face in youth and campus ministry, especially the retreat teams and Spirit Fire leadership teams—you are my inspiration. Thank you.

The leadership of the National Catholic Student Coalition also offered me immense support.

To Frank Cunningham and the editorial team at Ave Maria Press, thank you for believing in me and giving this book a chance.

The staff and faith community at Blessed John XXIII Catholic University Center have been a phenomenal witness of welcome and hospitality, offering a home away from home for students, and providing a powerful model of campus ministry between the Church and higher education. I am blessed to share in this community of seekers and believers. So many of you journey with me.

To 'Romey Gaudreau, my cyberspace wizard and late night instant messaging soul friend, I am so grateful.

My husband and son gift me with encouragement and patience, saying goodnight as I work into the wee hours or leave them to fend for themselves while I'm away leading retreats. Your love wraps me like a favorite quilt and sustains me, always.

And to the Holy One who always surprises me, may you blow where you will, and may I follow.

Introduction

There are as many ways to pray as there are
moments in life. Sometimes we seek out a
quiet spot and want to be alone, sometimes
we look for a friend and want to be together.
Sometimes we like a book, sometimes we
prefer music. Sometimes we want to sing
out with hundreds, sometimes only whisper
with a few. Sometimes we want to say it
with words, sometimes in deep silence. In all
these moments, we gradually make our lives
more of a prayer and we open our hands
to be led by God even to places we would
rather not go.

—HENRI J.M. NOUWEN[1]

This collection of personal prayer practices from Catholic college students was inspired by students at Blessed John XXIII Catholic University Center in Fort Collins, Colorado. Late one night, at a retreat planning meeting, I reflected with the student leadership team about how we all do little things that nurture our individual, distinctive relationships with God. They are those daily or weekly practices that we may not ever speak about to others.

I asked the team of ten students to e-mail me their prayer practices as part of their retreat preparation. Over the course of the next week, as I received their e-mails, I was incredibly inspired. Short paragraphs of grace allowed me a glimpse into the unique way we relate to God in very personal language and activity. My soul was touched through their reflections and personal practices.

At our next planning meeting, I told them how enthusiastic I was about their responses, and made known I thought they should be in a book form for others—especially those their own age—to also be inspired, and encourage reflection upon the ways we all express our unique relationships with God. Thus, this book was birthed, and now contains personal prayer practices from Catholic college students around the country. Contributions come from diverse geographical locations, with students studying at private, state, and community colleges, in a multiplicity of majors, each with a personal way to connect with God. Their reflections are designed to inspire, challenge, and motivate you to articulate and put into practice the daily "little things" that will bring you into deeper communication and union with God, family, Church, and world.

A primary developmental task for college-age men and women is to develop your own identity. This is reflected in the choices of intellectual pursuits, friendship connections, owning your religion, choosing a vocation (typically marriage and sometimes religious life), and serving others. These are years to explore what really excites you—what brings you energy and makes you excited about being alive. It is the time to name the dreams and desires of your heart and to seek them out. This is also the time to deepen your relationship with God.

These young-adult years are a time of transition in so many ways. Perhaps for the first time you are away from your family at college and the structures that you have known day in and day out. You have the freedom to make your own decisions—choices that can either be detrimental or life-giving. College can be a frightening and lonely time as you face life decisions and challenges to your beliefs and values from classmates, professors, and the dominant culture. But it can also be can be exhilarating, invigorating, and incredibly fruitful as you learn even more deeply what you care about and who you were created to be. Prayer can help you articulate who you are and allow you to nurture your God relationship.

People pray in many different ways—from solitude to active reflection to communal worship. What is important for you is that God comes to you in a specific time and place, and wants to be a part of your life here and now. God loves you no matter what and is never absent from you. Developing personal prayer practices help us be in relationship with our Creator, with all of God's creation through Jesus Christ, and in the Holy Spirit.

Use the prayer practices of others your age to contrast your prayer life with theirs. Pray along with your contemporaries using and adapting their ways to pray. If you are so inspired, adopt or create a new prayer practice! Some questions you may choose to think about on your own, with a friend, or in a small group include:

- **What are the personal things I do to connect with God?**

- **When and where do I experience God most profoundly in my life?**

- **How do I think of God? How has my understanding of God changed throughout my life?**

- **When is my favorite time of day? Why?**

- **How do I need God the most in my life?**

- **What are my deepest desires for my life?**

- **What "little things" can I do that will help me nurture my relationship with God?**

- **How much do I trust that God loves me no matter what?**

These are only some of the questions you can think about and answer for yourself. After each chapter, several other reflection questions are included.

God wants to be so much more than just a Sunday or occasional happening in your life. Your prayer practices will help keep your relationship with God vital, growing, and alive. It is the relationship that can make all the difference. It's never too early—or too late—in life to begin noticing how you can nurture your relationship with God. The importance of developing personal "prayer practices" to engage a God who is as interested in you at 4:00 a.m. while you are sleeping as he is while you are preparing for a big exam cannot be underestimated.

Before heading to college, locate a Catholic faith community where you will be living—and contact the campus minister before you arrive. Most campus ministers will mail you a welcome packet and be excited to personally meet with you. Many programs offer welcome week activities and perhaps a "newcomer's retreat" in the early fall.

If you are already away at college and haven't yet connected with a faith community, you have many resources available to you. Contact the Catholic Campus Ministry Association at www.ccmanet.org. On their website is a link to campus ministry programs around the country. And consider joining the National Catholic Student Coalition (more information at www.catholicstudent.org). Check out any Catholic student organizations through the student center at your college or university. And, if you still are stumped, e-mail me directly at: PrayerPractices@PeggeBernecker.com. I would be happy to connect you to a Catholic faith community near you.

I wish you blessings in your unique faith journey. It can be the most exciting adventure of your life.

Time Made Holy

God looked at everything he had made,
and he found it very good.

—GENESIS 1:31A

God created order in the world, making all time holy. Creation is an invitation to pay attention to God through the beauty of all the earth. It is an invitation for each of us to recognize the presence of God beyond Sunday Mass or in times of need. Intentionally engaging with "time made holy" involves noticing, appreciating, and entering into relationship with the world around us—the life we are living in the present.

Living authentically in time made holy requires discipline, a sense of humor, and learning to see with new eyes—eyes that are wide open to the wonders of the world and to God already present in our lives.

THERE are many different ways I connect with God throughout the day. First, in my car, when I can't find a good song on the radio, I just shut it off and spend some time in prayer. Second, often times when I am sitting in class and feeling impatient or having a hard time focusing, I will write a tiny little prayer in the margin of my notebook so small that I can barely read it myself. I always feel a sense of peace after expressing my frustration to God. Lastly, my favorite time with God is at night. Before I go to bed, I light a candle, turn off the lights, and share with God the contents of my day, and the contents of my heart.

Tessa S.
Senior, Ministry
Viterbo University, La Crosse, WI

I WEAR a very small cross necklace everyday. It is my constant reminder that Jesus is always with me. I pray for his guidance and protection every morning when I put it on. I reach for it and say a little prayer every time I catch myself sinning. I also start playing with it out of habit when I am nervous or upset. I eventually realize that I am doing this and then think of him and pray for his guidance and support. This has helped me immensely as I struggle to live my faith through the temptations of college and adulthood.

Laura R.
Senior, Pre-veterinary Medicine
Purdue University, West Lafayette, IN

EVERY day when I walk out my front door to my first class I am motivated to thank God for a new, beautiful day and ask him to bless everything I do and know that every act is an offering to him. We have bells that ring from our chapel on every hour. The bells remind me to say a little prayer. No matter where I am on campus, I look toward the chapel. It is in the center of campus and I am reminded to keep Christ in the center of my life. It's funny, but I find myself saying a prayer when I look at the clock and it is on the hour even when I'm not at school.

Elizabeth I.
Freshman, Occupational Therapy
Saint Ambrose University, Davenport, IA

FOR me, my prayer practice is simply the attitude I live with every day. It's kind of like a background meditation where I remind myself to slow down, to stay focused on what's happening here and now, to be mindful of my body and my soul and God's spirit. Prayer increases my patience, and I think it makes me a better Christian because I'm not always waiting for the "next thing." I can really pay attention to what God needs me to be doing, right now, whether it's according to my master plan or not.

Kathy G.
Senior, Philosophy
Purdue University, West Lafayette, IN

THROUGHOUT my day, I stop a few times to remember why I am really here. I have to take at least two minutes to breathe in and thank God for the day. I enjoy every aspect of life and realize the place I am in is so wonderful. To step back and take a look at my life is a prayer for me. It helps me stay grounded and realize how blessed I am by God. When I have more free time, I recite the Hail Mary and Our Father. I sometimes stop into one of the chapels at school to say quick prayers. I always try to remember God throughout my day.

Susan M.
Sophomore, Nursing
Saint Mary's College, Notre Dame, IN

I USED to feel guilty about not setting aside enough time to pray and just be with God.

I have realized, however, that I can talk to God anywhere and everywhere and it doesn't have to be elaborate or formal. These simple prayer practices help me connect with God among my ordinary daily tasks and events. Almost every morning I recite a Hail Mary with each strand of hair that I place in the curling iron. Also, running allows me to zone out the rest of the world and my body comes into a quiet rhythm. I take this opportunity to listen to God and focus on every breath that I take, thanking God for all of the blessings in my life.

Gina B.
Senior, Microbiology
Colorado State University, Fort Collins, CO

ONE of my favorite places to pray is among nature. I love living in Colorado where I can hike, ski, or mountain bike. Each one of these activities brings me closer to God as I enjoy the natural beauty he has created. Another thing I love to do is light a candle, dim the lights, and just be in God's presence. It is a wonderful reflection time for me and I receive so much clarity.

Emily P.
Senior, Psychology
Colorado State University, Fort Collins, CO

LIKE any other college student, finding time to exercise my faith is difficult. However, one way I attempt to do so is through prayer. I routinely say small prayers throughout the day, especially in gratitude for everything God has given to me. Although I don't always have time to stop what I'm doing to kneel and pray, I make time to smile at the first glimpse of the sun and the beginning of a new day. I find smiles, like prayers, bring joy to those who give them and to those who receive them.

Ashley O.
Freshman, International Business
Saint Mary's College, Notre Dame, IN

EVERY day when I'm driving from my house to school or work, I see my mountains, the beautiful Organ Mountains that God created! They remind me to thank God for the beautiful day.

Christen K.
Sophomore, Secondary Science Education
New Mexico State University, Las Cruces, NM

AS a busy college student, I do my best to incorporate God into my life in a variety of ways. There are many days where I don't feel that I can spend a great deal of time in meditation. So instead, I look for God in the simple parts of my day and praise him in everything that I do, large and small. I try to say a short prayer or read a devotional in the morning to start off my day. Later in the day, I say short little prayers. For example while walking through campus I will praise God for newly fallen snow or for seeing an old friend. Whenever I drive to work, I usually either pray a decade of the rosary or listen to Christian music. I've also found that I really enjoy praying the rosary during a walk or run. However, my favorite way to pray is to stop in at our Newman Center sporadically to pray in front of the Blessed Sacrament and to just talk to Jesus.

Kate H.
Sophomore, Business Marketing and Management
University of Nebraska, Lincoln, NE

SO life as a college student can be very hectic, right? Well I have found that the only way that I can survive the craziness of college is through my prayer rituals. In the morning when I put on my jeans, I slip my rosary ring into the right pocket so that I have it on me all day. Even if I don't get an opportunity to recite the rosary, I can rub it and focus better on my work. When the weather is nice, I walk eleven minutes down the road to a nearby lake and forest where I can reflect on my life and journal about my faith in God.

Catie F.
Sophomore, Social Work
Central Missouri State University,
Warrensburg, MO

For Further Reflection

- **How do I believe that God is interested in the details of my daily life?**

- **What are some times during my day that I can set aside for prayer?**

- **How can I make prayer a part of my current daily activities?**

- **How can I recognize God in the events of my day?**

Conversation with God

We pray in order to speak with God and to hear him
speak to us by inspirations and movements in the
interior of our soul. And generally this is with a very deli-
cious pleasure, because it is a great good for us to speak to
so great a Lord; and when he answers he spreads abroad
a thousand precious balms and unguents, which give great
sweetness to the soul.
—SAINT FRANCIS DE SALES[2]

Talking to friends, listening intently, and telling our life stories is how we learn about one another and what we value. God desires the same type of conversation with us! God hopes for a profound friendship with each of us, and is attentive to us as if we were the only person that mattered at any given time.

In fact, God is always waiting for us whenever we speak or listen to him. As with any close friend, a daily, ongoing conversation or a structured time of sharing with God will nurture a life-defining friendship. The divine conversation we cultivate today and tomorrow will span all the days of our lives.

"HELLO? Hello? Anybody there?"
After years of hanging up on him midway
through prayer while lying in bed at night, and
letting the sandman bring me a dream rather
than finishing my conversation with God, I fig-
ured I needed a new strategy for connecting
with the Lord.

So there I was walking to my next engage-
ment of the day, with the sun high in the sky and
me between tasks, in conversation with God
about where and when I should or could share
my time with him. I answered my own question.
Anywhere, anytime, but preferably during the
times I am walking about.

Now I always look forward to walking
because it is my prayer time. From my porch to
the mailbox, from the doors of the store to my
car in the parking lot, from class on campus to
the bus stop, I am walking in conversation with
God. God really comes alive for me when I walk
with him. I can find a real connection in my daily
jaunts with the One who blesses my entire life's
journey.

Elizabeth H.
Senior, Landscape Horticulture
Colorado State University, Fort Collins, CO

RECENTLY I have noticed how impatient I can get during the day. One day, while waiting for my e-mail to load, I decided to say a prayer. It was wonderful. I felt better after praying and before I knew it, my e-mail was waiting for me. So now, whenever I am waiting in line or waiting for someone or something, I use the precious moments to talk to God. When I do this I feel that God is always right beside me.

Nicole P.
Sophomore, Dietetics
Iowa State University, Ames, IA

I WILL be walking across campus or sitting outside somewhere and I will silently say, "Okay, God. Here I am. What is your will?" And then it is up to me to listen. Listening to God is a broad activity. One can never know how God will respond. It can be through the words or actions of other people, through the birds, through the weather, through a chance meeting, or even through a strong thought. It is difficult at first to decipher when God is speaking and what he is saying, but it becomes much clearer with practice and trust. Once I hear what I believe to be God's words, I must act—without action, prayer is pointless.

Jeremy R.
Sophomore, Photography
Central Missouri State College,
Warrensburg, MO

I PICK out a point of reference on campus or on a route I drive often, and whenever I pass that point I say a little prayer. For example, whenever I walk past this one beautiful oak tree I just turn my thoughts to God. If I am with someone else when I walk past the oak tree I pray for them. It is amazing the things that come to your mind to pray about when you just open up your heart to God. Another thing I do sometimes before I fall asleep is to go through the alphabet and list the qualities of God from A to Z. It really helps me to put things into perspective.

Ann-Marie Y.
Sophomore, History
Texas A & M University, College Station, TX

IF I'm having a bad day, or going through a difficult time in my life, I often stop myself and realize that God is watching over me. He takes care of my hurts. He accepts me for who I am. God understands that I am trying my hardest to be everything he has made me to be. I am his child and he lives in me. After that time of remembrance and understanding, I feel as if I can continue throughout my day because God believes in me, and he knows I'm doing my best.

Stephanie B.
Senior, Sociology and Social Work
Saint Joseph's College of Maine,
Standish, ME

I THINK something unique that I do is pray in Spanish. I don't do it a whole lot, but when I do it is a way of making me more conscious of what I'm saying to God. It also allows me to look for different ways of saying things that get redundant other times when I'm praying. Also, I really like to pray when I ride my mountain bike. I thank God for the beauty that surrounds me. Or sometimes I get on my bike with a big problem over my head and just say to God that I'm going to ride and not think about it too much. Back when I had just graduated from high school and was a new freshman, I had a lot of anxiety and was dealing with a broken heart. My bike really helped me to "ride away" from that stuff and feel a little better.

Abraham W.
Junior, Biology with a minor in Spanish
Colorado State University, Fort Collins, CO

A PRIEST once told me that when you need God to be by your side recite "Come, Lord Jesus!" and he will be with you. Ever since I heard this, I find myself saying it all the time—for safety, for guidance, and to give thanksgiving. Just knowing Jesus is by my side is enough to get me through the hardest of days.

Lucy O.
Junior, Photography
Central Missouri State College,
Warrensburg, MO

I OFTEN feel especially close to God after talking to my parents on the phone. Like many people, I have a tendency to think about God as grand and powerful, only concerned with my major life events and sum total virtue. A conversation with my parents reminds me that my heavenly Mother/Father is ready to listen to my small problems as well as large ones. I can imagine God taking motherly care that I'm dressing warmly, or rejoicing as my dad would in my emerging political consciousness. Even when there's nagging from my parents involved, a call home always gives me cause to thank God for my family, who model God's multitudinous grace.

Kate W.
Junior, Psychology
Harvard College, Cambridge, MA

WE all have hectic schedules, so anytime I can free myself to chat with God, I do. It really isn't anything planned. Most of the time I just find a quiet place to sit where I am not focusing on anything else but God. If the day is good for me I celebrate with him. I thank him for all that he has blessed me with. If life seems a bit tough, I tell God my troubles and worries and ask for his strength and guidance. That's it. Sounds simple I know, but it is wonderful. We have our own quiet and peaceful conversation. I talk to him and he graciously listens. In the end, though problems may not be solved, I always feel refreshed and renewed.

Fredrick Q.
Senior, Psychology
Colorado State University, Fort Collins, CO

IN my experience with prayer, I have found that my life-changing revelations have come more from listening to God than speaking to him. Sometimes I've found that the thing I hear from God is not what I hoped for, not what I wanted most, but what I needed.

Megan W.
Freshman, Business Finance and Economics
Iowa State University, Ames, IA

For Further Reflection

- How do I talk to God throughout the day as a friend?

- What is happening in my life that God would like to hear about from me?

- What are some of the ways I have found that God speaks to me in prayer?

- How can I become a better listener when I pray?

Gratitude

If the only prayer you say in your life is "thank you,"
that would suffice.

—MEISTER ECKHART[3]

Living with a grateful heart means experiencing God as the source of all life. A grateful heart takes joy in the goodness and beauty of our world. When we recognize the gifts of life—be they in struggle or delight—and learn to offer thanksgiving for each moment, we are blessed and become a blessing to ourselves and others. A grateful heart has an increased capacity to love. Imagine a world where gratitude is practiced moment by moment with an awareness of the gift of life. In such a world peace could become a concrete reality.

TO be honest, my relationship with God mostly resembles a roller coaster; some days I feel really close to him, and on others I let him take a back seat to things I treat as more important. Lately, though, I am more aware of the blessings in my life—be they large or small—and offer a simple "Thank You" to the Lord. It doesn't seem like much, but it gives me an opportunity to appreciate all he has done and continues to do for me while letting him know I haven't set him aside in my priorities.

Kaitlin G.
Junior, Spanish and English Education
Colorado State University, Fort Collins, CO

THIS may sound silly, but I use my sneezes as reminders to thank God in the middle of my day. When I sneeze and no one is around to say "God bless you," I just take a moment to think about one of the specific ways God has already blessed me. I often sneeze as I walk out into the bright sun after a class. I thank God for the beautiful sky or for anything else that comes to mind. I find it's a great way to remember to thank God regularly in addition to my frequent petitions, which seem to come more naturally.

Timothy H.
Senior, Physics
Rice University, Houston, TX

ONE thing that I do several times a day is to give a wink and a smile up to heaven when something beautiful happens and I actually notice. For example, maybe I'm driving around, and I happen to look at the mountains and see how beautiful they are—a wink and a smile. Or if I see a very loving family in a store or on the street, I give God a wink and a smile. It's kind of weird, I guess, but it's what I do.

Joel C.
Junior, Political Science
Colorado State University, Fort Collins, CO

MY favorite prayers are what

I like to call my popcorn prayers. These are prayers or thank-yous that I give to God sporadically throughout the day. Whether I have a friend in need, something good happens to me, or he's helped me avoid a bad accident, I will offer a short prayer. I call them popcorn prayers because I don't set a time to say them and they don't occur all at the same time, but I think that God enjoys them just the same. I consider them God's snack for the day. I love having a bag of popcorn as a snack between meals and I am sure God appreciates it when I offer him my short popcorn prayers as a snack.

Rebecca H.
Freshman, Spanish
University of Nebraska, Lincoln, NE

ONE Lent, I decided to add

something to my prayer life instead of giving up some food item. I liked the idea of saying "Thank you" to God whenever something went wrong, not right. I hoped it would bring me closer to Jesus and his suffering. It was a difficult task during those forty days, but I have continued to do it. I still look up to God and say "Thank you" every time someone cuts me off on the road, every time a friend or a family member goes into the hospital, and every time I experience something that might seem negative at first.

Christopher R.
Graduate Student, Secondary English
Education
University of Memphis, Memphis, TN

ONE of the things that I do to remind myself of God's goodness is to stop throughout the day to thank him for the little things that he gives me. For example, if at any point in the day I see something that puts a smile on my face—like a kid eating an ice cream cone or little old ladies laughing with each other over coffee—I will stop and say a short prayer of thanksgiving, because I know that it was God who put that child or those ladies there to make me smile.

Emily P.
Sophomore, Audiology and Speech Pathology
Fresno State University, Fresno, CA

PRAYING to God is about more than just guidance and help . . . it's also about thanksgiving! Before a test or a big project is due, everyone prays to God for help getting a good grade. After I finish the project, I try to give thanks to God for helping me through it, whether I did my best or didn't do so well. Whenever life gets busy and stress mounts, I take a step back and pray to God. Hopefully waiting that extra few seconds helps me realize that whatever needs to get done or whatever is stressing me out isn't all that important, but it will get done through the help and guidance of God.

George S.
Senior, Electrical Engineering and Computer Science
New Mexico Tech, Socorro, NM

OVER the course of my first year here at college, I've had a really tough time trying to get a set prayer schedule. Not praying regularly has been a constant source of frustration. But this Lent I realized that whenever we hear of Jesus' prayer life in the Bible, it is as if he is just conversing one to one with his Father. I realized that this is the kind of prayer for me right now. So I've stopped worrying so much about structure, and I've tried to stop feeling guilty if I fall asleep at night without praying. In exchange, now I try to say "thank you" to God every time something good happens and especially when something bad happens. I talk to him on my way to class and when I'm laughing at myself for whatever silly mistake I've made in the day. I'm trying to create a friendship with God instead of a schedule.

Wendy W.
Freshman, Child, Adult, and Family Services
Iowa State University, Ames, IA

IN my busy life, sometimes it
is a struggle to fit prayer time into my day.
Something that has greatly helped me is to
create a prayer space in my apartment. I have
taken the mantel above my fireplace and draped
it with cloth and prayer shawls. Around the
mantel I have a dozen candles. I have filled the
wall above the mantel with pictures and images
of people who are important to me and whom I
am thankful for: my family, friends, and the youth
who I have ministered to. I have about thirty
pictures up there! I also have pictures of saints
and heroes of faith all over the mantel as well as
notes from people I have attended retreats with
as part of campus ministry. What I love about
my prayer space is that it serves as a reminder
to me to thank God for all of the blessings in my
life. It also helps me realize that I have encoun-
tered Christ through my many friends and my
loving family.

But my favorite way to pray is through
rhythm. I have been a drummer for eleven years,
and one of my favorite drums is my Djembe,
which is an African drum. In the evenings I love
taking my drum and creating a simple rhythm, to
where it feels like my heart is beating that same

rhythm. Then I take the rhythm and change it slightly, and really allow myself to become lost in that rhythm. That's when I begin to be intentional with my prayer. I first offer prayers of thanksgiving, and then I move toward prayers asking for strength, wisdom, patience, and trust in the situations where I need them. Sometimes I sing or chant more traditional prayers over the rhythm such as the Our Father or Hail Mary. To me it is an awesome experience to allow music to be an avenue of prayer.

Jeromey G.
Junior, Computer Information Systems
Colorado State University, Fort Collins, CO

FIRST I always put my shoes under my bed. That way when I wake up in the morning I have to hit my knees, and while I'm down there I can pray! I always talk to God about how very grateful I am for everything he has given me. Getting on my knees in the morning and at night really humbles me. In the morning I pray to prepare myself for the upcoming day. At night I thank God for the gifts he's given me. It's the perfect start and end to every day.

Christopher H.
Junior, Public Relations
Long Island University, Brookville, NY

For Further Reflection

- What am I most grateful for in my life?

- Who is someone who inspires me to pray in thanksgiving?

- What is a prayer of gratitude that I can say to myself each day?

- When are times I say "thanks" to God for his blessings? How so?

Catholic Traditions

*It is not to remain in a golden ciborium that He comes to us
each day from heaven; it's to find another heaven, infinitely
more dear to Him than the first: the heaven of our soul,
made to His image, the living temple of the adorable Trinity!*

——Saint Thérèse of Lisieux[4]

We discover rich wisdom and grace in our Catholic prayer traditions. Whether we worship at Mass, finger prayer beads with a familiar Hail Mary, sit before the Blessed Sacrament, pray a novena, gaze at an icon of Christ, or enter into the deep mystical prayer tradition of the Church, we ultimately enlarge the "heaven of our soul." Through Catholic devotions we become more loving, prayerful, and compassionate, knowing God by experience both personally and in the long history of our family of faith.

WHEN I was making my First Communion in second grade, the priest gave everyone a simple white beaded rosary. I still keep that rosary in my purse and whenever I'm feeling stressed I run my fingers over it. Right before major exams or finals, I'll arrive a little early and pray the rosary while I'm waiting to begin. It helps clear my mind and focuses me on the task at hand. I've had it for so long that the shiny plastic beads have dulled to a pencil-lead gray and some of the beads have become chipped. However, that's my rosary and I wouldn't want another.

Amy W.
Freshman, Pharmacy
Purdue University, West Lafayette, IN

AT my university, we are blessed to have a beautiful Virgin Mary grotto. While passing this grotto each day, I say a Hail Mary and ask my Mother to lead me to her Son.

Patrick O.
Sophomore, Marketing
Saint Ambrose University, Davenport, IA

SOMETHING I do but don't usually tell people is that I carry a mini prayerbook in my pocket when I'm taking a test. I also always have rosary beads in a pouch in my backpack. And I never travel without having them with me.

Christie M.
Junior, Biology
Colorado State University, Fort Collins, CO

AFTER receiving Communion, while
everyone is praying quietly, I take the time to
truly talk to God. I hold onto my pearl rosary, so
heavy and cool to the touch. Its articulation and
precision reminds me of all the beauty of creation that God made so carefully and lovingly.
I close my eyes, let the world slip away, and
allow myself to react with facial expressions to
any thoughts I want to share with God, whether
they be remorse (sad face) or joy (a smile). I let
myself go for five minutes of meditation, sing
along to the meditation song when I know it, and
truly spend quality time with God.

Kimanh N.
Senior, Psychology
University of Southern California,
Los Angeles, CA

I GO to Mass every morning and offer my day to God. Before making a major decision, like looking for a new academic advisor, I say the Divine Mercy novena for nine days. If I am able to complete it, then everything works fine. If I miss the novena on any day, I drop the plans.

Saju A.
Graduate Student, Electrical Engineering
University of Arizona, Tucson, AZ

DUE to our human condition, we all struggle with living out purity in mind, body, and heart to some extent. To help strengthen my will and get a little extra grace, I say three Hail Marys after receiving Our Lord in the Eucharist everyday. The power of prayer at that time is amazing!

> Corissa B.
> Junior, Theology
> Ave Maria College, Ypsilanti, MI

I FIND that I reach out to Jesus
when I've had a bad day or am in need of a
spiritual boost. I'll stop just inside the doorway
of the Newman Center chapel and stand there,
letting Jesus' presence fill my soul. During Lent I
made the effort to pray in front of the tabernacle
every day for ten minutes. Sometimes it was
inconvenient because I had to go out of my way
to stop at a church on Saturday and during the
week I would be in a hurry, but after a while if I
skipped a day I would really miss not spending
my ten quiet minutes with God. Since Easter, I
haven't been visiting the Blessed Sacrament as
regularly, but I do turn to God for conversation
as I walk to class or drive home.

Heather Q.
Senior, Environmental Science
University of California at Riverside,
Riverside, CA

AS a busy non-traditional student, working full time, I don't have much time for formal prayer. I do try to pay attention to God in the details that greet me each day of my life—in people, studies, the ocean stretching to the horizon, and meals with friends. Also, once a month our church has an hour of Adoration of the Blessed Sacrament for young adults. It's one of my favorite hours of the month when I enter into the candlelit stillness to become more present to the Real Presence.

Meg E.
Senior, English
University of California at Irvine, Irvine, CA

I TRY to make everything that I do (classes, homework, spending time with friends, etc.) a prayer! Prayer is how I get through my days at Creighton University. It's a difficult school, but prayer has helped. Without God, my love of the Church, and prayer, my life would just be completely empty!

Rebekah W.
Junior, Theology and Social Work
and Youth Ministry
Creighton University, Omaha, NE

ON a campus that constantly and
directly criticizes Christianity in everything from
the school newspaper to classroom discussions,
it is easy to allow feelings of alienation from
the overall student body and pessimism of the
state of the world in general to cloud one's daily
thoughts. For me, praying is one of the only ways
to cope. It seems next to impossible sometimes
with exams, term papers, and worrying about
what I am going to do with my life when I graduate, but twenty minutes of prayer a day can go
a long way. What I try to do is to sit or kneel
(depending on my mood) in front of a candle-lit
icon that illustrates the face of Christ. I usually
start with a couple of formal prayers, but I try
to end in silence, letting God speak to me and
help me sort out the true desires of my heart. By
committing myself to daily prayer, I am not only
reminded of what Christ has done for my fellow
students and myself, but also how I am called
to act toward my fellow students: as his humble
servant.

John-Paul P.
Senior, Political Science and International Affairs
University of California at Riverside,
Riverside, CA

THIS is a prayer practice that has a basic outline that can be varied every time and become unique to the individual. The prayer has the acronym ACTS—Adoration, Confession, Thanksgiving, and Supplication. First, you *adore* Christ—sing your favorite church song to praise him. Or you can go to an adoration chapel. You can also simply just pray words of worship. Next is *confession*, when you review your past sins and how you can do better. Also, you can go the extra step and celebrate the sacrament of reconciliation. Next is *thanksgiving*, simply thanking God for all the wonderful gifts you have been given. Lastly, is *supplication*, asking God to watch over specific instances in your life and the lives of those around you (these are like petitions at Mass). I like how it guides my prayer along, and it is easy to do before bed or while taking walks on campus. The acronym ACTS is a helpful way to remember the four steps. I can't take credit for creating this outline but I know how much it has guided my prayer life!

Jennifer C.
Sophomore, Family Studies
University of Arizona, Tucson, AZ

AFTER every Mass I attend, while genuflecting, I say this simple prayer, "Help!" It's amazing what it has done for me!

Sherrie Ann V.
Junior, Biological Sciences
Colorado State University, Fort Collins, CO

For Further Reflection

- What traditional Catholic devotions have been most fruitful in my own life?

- What is a Catholic devotion I would like to learn more about and incorporate into my prayer life?

- Is there a parent, relative, or friend that I could ask to share their experiences of Catholic prayer with me?

- What is the purpose of praying with traditional Catholic prayers or devotions?

Engaging Bodily Presence

The more attentive you are, and the longer you remain in a landscape, the more you will be embraced by its presence. Though you may be completely alone there, you know you're not on your own.

—JOHN O'DONOHUE[5]

The earth is clothed in God's grandeur, and as physical beings we enter into relationship with the world through our body and senses. We notice, smell, sweat, see, breathe, taste, touch, and listen to all of God's creation. It's no small wonder our bodies feel more alive when we take a walk or run, notice the colors that paint the world, feel the coolness of running water, or let the wind caress our skin. We also enter into a relationship with a God who took on a human body and experienced the same bodily sensations as we do. When we notice and engage our senses, we encounter a landscape that goes beyond the visible and enters the invisible recesses of our being. Nature and our own unique body allow us to embrace and be embraced by the author of creation.

I USUALLY go for a short run in the morning, just to wake myself up. I enjoy the sunrise and the quiet before the day really begins. This had been my routine for almost a year. One morning I was running past the pond at City Park. There was a mist blanketing the water. The ducks and geese were stretching their wings and fishing for breakfast. I had been thinking about all the things I had to do that day and was becoming quite overwhelmed. Then I looked up and suddenly the world stopped. Everything that I had been stressing over left my mind and what was left I will never forget. I felt and saw the presence of God around me in this waking world. It was as if I had been looking through dirty, finger-smudged glasses, and he had suddenly cleaned them for me. Everything around me looked so new, like it was the first time I had ever seen anything. My morning became anything but routine. Now the mornings are my favorite time to run not just because the sunrise looks pretty, but because I know I am sharing a moment just between me and God.

Aimee L.
Junior, Biology with a minor in Anatomy and Neurobiology
Colorado State University, Fort Collins, CO

I BELIEVE there are many ways of praising the Lord without reciting prayers (although these work too). I love popping in some of my favorite Christian songs and just soaking up the words and thinking about how God has blessed my life. I'm a college track athlete and for me running has become a spiritual experience. I like to look up at the ceiling right before I take off for a long jump approach and remember that he is with me or incorporate Christian music into the beats of my steps when I'm on a long run.

Michelle P.
Senior, Behavioral Science
Mount Marty College, Yankton, SD

I AM very involved in choir and dance. I love to do both things and I incorporated them as a form of prayer. I sing God's praises and have been told that singing is "praying twice." Through dancing I can use my whole self to pray to God instead of just using my words. I do spend quiet times with God, reading the Bible and talking with him, but sometimes it is just easier to tell God what I am feeling by dancing and singing—so that is what I do!

Sarah M.
Freshman, Psychology and Theater
Saint Mary's College, Notre Dame, IN

I GO to City Park and take off my

shoes and breathe deeply and sink my toes in the sand while I dangle my feet off a swing. Then I pump the swing using my whole body to get as high as I can. Then I lean back, look up at the sky, and talk to God. From doing this and looking at the sky, I have come to believe that God really likes the color blue. Some days I spend hours on the swing just talking to God. I rarely stop swinging when I still feel sad, bitter, or afraid. I even go to the swings when I am really in a good mood just to thank God for such a wonderful day! I think this ritual works so well for me because I am able to involve all my senses and put my body in its favorite place, as a child before the Lord.

Sarah B.
Graduate Student, Curriculum and Instruction;
Initial Professional Teacher Education
Program with an endorsement in Education for
the Linguistically Different
University of Colorado at Denver, Denver, CO

A SPECIFIC time when I feel especially in tune with God is when I am at high altitudes, and so growing up in Colorado essentially has made me a more religious person, I believe. In my hometown of Grand Junction, there is a place called Dinosaur Hill where I am able to climb to the top, see the whole valley, and just converse with God about all that concerns me. I seem to find answers to all of my questions when I am up there. It is in this state of euphoria that I can center myself to begin my journey again, as I set out on the path back down the hill.

Heidi B.
Senior, Biology with Teacher Education
Mesa State College, Grand Junction, CO

ONE of the times I pray is when
I just sit and take in the beauty around me on
campus: a squirrel hiding nuts, a child playing
in the leaves, or a friendly smile from a passing student. During the winter months, my time
alone with God while walking (however quickly)
from class to class takes on a whole new meaning. I breathe in deeply, allowing the sharp, brisk
air to fill my lungs, reflecting on how the Holy
Spirit fills my soul every day with a new appre-
ciation for the life that God provides. I arrive at
my next class with a feeling of warmth, one that
stays with me all day.

Elizabeth B.
Junior, Cultural Anthropology and Social
Science
University of Michigan, Ann Arbor, MI

MY spiritual practices: going for a long run in nature somewhere, talking with a friend, and sitting quietly somewhere and just being.

Jacob M.
Senior, Wildlife Biology
Colorado State University, Fort Collins, CO

WINTER, spring, summer, and
fall are all just the perfect occasions to take a
walk and pray outside. Taking just a half an hour
to an hour out of my day to take a walk brings
me serenity and the chance to think and pray.
With little noise and the presence of God's natural creation, it's so wonderful to forget about
stress and remember God.

> Abbey F.
> Junior, Public Relations
> Loras College, Dubuque, IA

I SEE the beauty of God's creation in the little things each day. While walking to class, I'll see the sun bouncing off the brick buildings, creating a color that just can't be found anywhere else. I feel a sense of warmth and security that I know can only come from God. When it is warm, I love to just sit still underneath the towering oak trees. Even though there are people dashing about all around me, I feel that I am sitting alone with God, simply listening as he speaks to my heart.

Marie W.
Freshman, Theology
Saint Ambrose University, Davenport, IA

I WAS born and raised in a tiny community in central Minnesota where trees and lakes far outnumbered cars and buildings, so it's no wonder I experience God in a deeper way when I am outdoors. And when no one's around, sometimes I even take to kneeling in the flowers and the grass in prayer, just as if they were pews in a church. Maybe it's silly, but I'd like to think that God enjoys me taking so much delight in his creation.

Karen S.
Senior, Zoology
University of Wisconsin, Madison, WI

For Further Reflection

- When are occasions when my body and senses feel most in tune with God?

- What is my special place in nature where I am most attentive to God's presence?

- What are specific ways I notice God's presence

    —in my breathing?

    —with my sight?

    —in a fragrance?

    —through my hearing?

    —in something I touch?

    —in a favorite food?

Love One Another

The tender mercy of God has given us one another.

—Catherine McAuley[6]

At the Last Supper, Jesus gave his disciples a new commandment: "As I have loved you, so you also should love one another. This is how all will know that you are my disciples, if you have love for one another" (Jn 13:34–35). Our actions and attitude flow from the depth of our commitment to that simple imperative: love one another. In our prayer, we contemplate a God who is love. Through this relationship, we bring life-giving action to others. When we love, we experience life in abundance. Also, when we pray for others, even our enemies, we bring a healthy, healing love to those relationships and to the world at large.

ONE way I pray on a daily basis is by spontaneously praying for people I pass by during the course of the day. For example, if someone goes out of their way to hold the door for me while I'm frantically rushing to class, I pray that that person is blessed with an abundance of graces throughout the day for their kind gesture. However, I also pray for people even if they act rudely. I do this because I realize that everyone has bad days, and that even those who have hurt or offended me deserve the chance to experience God's love. Praying for people I see in passing provides me with an opportunity to both support the body of Christ in action and to further Christ's kingdom on earth. We may never realize how much a quick prayer may lift a person's spirits. As Saint Paul wrote: "Do not neglect hospitality, for through it some have unknowingly entertained angels" (Heb 13:2).

Nina M.
Sophomore, Nursing
University of Pennsylvania, Philadelphia, PA

AS a student, I spend much of my time walking or riding the bus to class. So I take those times to pray. I often find inspiration for prayers from others who I meet on my journeys to class. They tend to shine a light in areas that I've not thought about before. For example, if I'm having a rough day and someone goes out of their way to help me, I offer thanks to God for this positive event. Or if I see a mother and a child, I say a prayer that they have a wonderful day together. These short prayers are ways to remember how everyone we meet has an effect on our lives.

Justin V.
Senior, Civil Engineering
University of Michigan, Ann Arbor, MI

I CURRENTLY have a field placement in an extremely poor and high crime neighborhood in the South Bronx, Mott Haven. I work in a homeless shelter for men with mental illness and substance abuse problems. Needless to say I sometimes experience feelings of frustration, confusion, sadness, helplessness, and guilt. However, instead of letting these negative emotions come between me and the Lord, I have come to realize the importance of finding harmony among the chaos. Down the street a few blocks I have located Saint Luke's Catholic Church, better known to the community as Iglesia San Lucas. The beautiful historic church was built in 1897 when the Bronx was a wilderness. Although getting to the church sometimes means going outside of my comfort zone, I am amazed at the warmth I feel and the blanket of peace I am covered with when I step into the church. Mostly it is very quiet in the church. I sometimes hear the children playing during their recess at the adjoining Catholic school, and on occasion there are Spanish- speaking nuns in the church arranging exquisite fresh flowers. Many times I sit quietly in the front pew staring in awe at the massive crucifix that hangs before me as I allow my thoughts and prayers to flood from my soul. Other times I kneel in concentrated prayer. Or I light a prayer candle among the many burning flames. Or I quietly sing to the Lord. Sometimes I visit with a nun in Spanish. Regardless of how I lift my prayers, being able to find the quiet, powerful presence of our Lord in the midst of a hectic neighborhood that is not my home encourages me to recognize the beauty in uncommon places and fills me with the love and strength of the Lord that he might shine through me to others.

Christie H.
Graduate Student, Social Work
Columbia University, New York, NY

ONE form of prayer I commonly

use is quiet meditation while thinking about special people in my life. I allow visions of my friends and family to enter my mind, and then I think about why I love them and offer up a short prayer of thanksgiving for their presence in my life.

Sarah D.
Senior, Health and Exercise Science
Colorado State University, Fort Collins, CO

ONE person I pray for on a daily basis is my future spouse. I pray that, whoever he is, God will touch his life and help him to grow in all things. I also ask our Blessed Mother to keep him safe and to give both of us the grace to know each other when we meet. This has been one of the most fruitful parts of my prayer life.

Danielle H.
Sophomore, Philosophy and Business
Boston College, Chestnut Hill, MA

I WOULDN'T consider myself to

be a "prayerful" person. I don't have a routine
prayer that I say, or a certain time set out in my
day to pray. However, I do feel that there are
little things that I do randomly every day to bring
me closer to God. When I volunteer my time
with the Church, or in the community, or when I
go out of my way to be courteous and compassionate to others, I feel that that I am praying.
Sometimes when I have to be nice to someone
that I would consider to be an enemy, I say a
little prayer to myself: "God give me patience
and strength to help me be a better person, and
to serve God's kingdom." To me, that is prayer
enough for now.

Nicole L.
Junior, Public Relations
Colorado State University, Fort Collins, CO

"TO love another person is to see the face of God." This is a key foundation of my personal prayer life. By loving others, I see them for who they truly are: God's own. I see how God is within them, guiding them, and helping them. When the world seems to say that my fellow brothers and sisters are insignificant and small, I continue to look for their greatness. By loving others and seeing God in them, I make my prayer one of thanksgiving and then allow God to work through me as well.

Daniel M.
Freshman, English Education
Saint Ambrose University, Davenport, IA

I SOMETIMES say little prayers
for people when I am talking with them online
and they tell me something about their day
that strikes me as something that I should pray
about. At night when I'm trying to fall asleep I
pray for my friends and the rest of the events in
my life.

Andrea S.
Sophomore, Pharmacy
Butler University, Indianapolis, IN

I FIND that I have started praying more since going to college. I give thanks to God every day for the skills that I have been given, especially those that allow me to work with older adults. I also find myself saying prayers for others in need. My fourth grade teacher taught us that when we hear sirens, we should say a prayer for the safety of the workers as well as the health and safety of those that they are going to help. I've tried to keep that habit as well.

Kirsten F.
Senior, Social Work
College of Saint Scholastica, Duluth, MN

I was walking through the

woods with my friend and noticed that someone
had spray-painted "pray" on the bridge of an
old train track. I felt as if it was a sign to pray,
so I asked my friend if he wanted to. Then he
said something that I will never forget. He said,
"I'm praying with my eyes open." Since then,
although I do pray in many other ways, I have
been praying with the eyes of my soul and heart
opened. The most beautiful prayers are those
given for other people.

Marcia L.
Junior, Environmental Science
with a minor in Geology
University of Michigan, Ann Arbor, MI

For Further Reflection

- Some of the ways I express my love for the people closest to me are. . . .

- What do I find the most difficult about loving others?

- Who are some people on the outskirts of my life who need my love? How will I provide my love for them?

- Write a prayer for someone with a special need.

Words: Written, Read, Sung

In the beginning was the Word,
*   and the Word was with God,*
*   and the Word was God.*
He was in the beginning with God.
All things came to be through him,
*   and without him nothing came to be.*
What came to be through him was life,
*   and this life was the light of the human race;*
the light shines in the darkness,
*   and the darkness has not overcome it.*

—JOHN 1:1–5

Engaging with the word of God in Scripture and other spiritual reading, including songs, provides words for us to listen to as we pray. We encounter the inspired Scripture through deliberate and meditative reading. We also find deep solace in God's word when we sing or listen to a song with inspiring lyrics or read from classic literature. Sometimes we can communicate with God through journaling. When we write our thoughts and prayers and then read them back in quiet reflection, we gain further insight into ourselves and into God.

I LIKE to set aside a specific time of day just for God and myself, usually at night right before I go to bed. I take my Bible, a notebook, and a pen and curl up in my pajamas and just read his word. I ask myself and God how I can apply what I've read. I usually write down my prayer because it helps me to stay focused and it keeps my mind from wandering. I like to make up stuff as I go and really just have a conversation with God. For me, this journaling with God helps to put things into perspective and gives me a more optimistic outlook on life.

Jodi D.
Senior, Human Service Counseling
Wayne State College, Wayne, NE

ON a daily basis, I try to write in my journal five things that I am grateful for. The items on the list vary from a phone call from a friend, to the safety of my brother serving in the military overseas, to having red Jell-O® at the cafeteria for dinner. Writing five things I am thankful for allows me to focus on the really big things in life and on the little things too. When a day seems really hard, focusing on five things I have to be grateful for is sometimes a challenge, but doing so helps me realize how truly blessed I am. I always end up whispering thank you to God as I put my journal away.

Therese W.
Junior, Speech Pathology
Saint John's University, New York, NY

I TAKE time usually every night to put on some music, read some Scripture, and write down my prayers. I write down whatever may be on my mind, and any intentions that I have.

Sylvia W.
Senior, Microbiology with a minor in Physics
Colorado State University, Fort Collins, CO

ONE of the ways that I continue
my relationship with God is through journaling.
I write letters to God. I write about my feelings,
thoughts, and dreams. I also read spiritual books
and try to spend time every day writing about
the things I see that remind me of God. One day
it was about all the migrating monarch butter-
flies that landed on my hand and arms during
a hike. Another time I wrote about the colors
of the sunset reflecting on the bay water near
the rock in Morro Bay that I see from my window. College is a hard time for me, and it makes
prayer more tangible for me if I put into words
my observations and conversations with God.
Then I don't feel so lonely.

Margaret K.
Sophomore, Fashion Merchandising
Cuesta Community College,
San Luis Obispo, CA

JOURNALING gives me a tangible way to pray. It clears my mind because I am more able to sort out my thoughts by writing them down. I enjoy praying the rosary because I feel closer to Christ during this time. It always fills me with a sense of peace.

Elizabeth S.
Freshman, Spanish
Saint Mary's College, Notre Dame, IN

WHEN praying to God, sometimes I find myself rambling on about other things instead of praying what is on my heart. Or, often times I will find my mind drifting off onto something else. I'm more focused when I write. Sometimes my prayers to God involve writing letters to him in a journal. Also, in this way, I'm able to re-read what I put down on paper and I'm not distracted by other incoming thoughts.

Melissa R.
Sophomore, Undeclared
Colorado State University, Fort Collins, CO

I OFTEN find myself in conversation with God through song. I love listening to a Christian CD or "church music" and just drifting away and really concentrating on the words. Often times, while on a walk, I will get a song stuck in my head. As weird as it sounds, I try to think about what those lyrics mean and how they relate to what I am praying about at that moment. Often times, I feel like I really find deep meaning in those lyrics and find answers to my prayers.

Maureen M.
Junior, Elementary Education
University of Delaware, Newark, DE

ONE of my favorite prayers is the Prayer of Saint Francis. After receiving communion, I always recite this prayer to myself. It helps me to remember the awesome sacrifice that Jesus made for me, and it helps me to remember things that I can do for others. It is a beautiful prayer, and it helps me to focus on what is really important—the giving rather than receiving, the pardoning if we are injured, and the forgiving of others so we may be forgiven.

Jean W.
Junior, Nursing
University of Arizona, Tucson, AZ

I USE the published prayer method *Miracle Hour* by Linda Schubert for my own prayer. The method breaks down an hour into five minute segments starting with praise, song, spiritual warfare, surrender, release of the Holy Spirit, repentance, forgiveness, scripture reflections, waiting for the Lord to speak, intercessions, petitions, and thanksgiving. Each section has a list of suggested scripture readings. It is designed to be used as the spirit moves you. At times I pray just one section; at others I use the entire pamphlet. It has bestowed amazing graces and sustained me during my greatest trials.

Bernadette O.
Sophomore, Economics
Columbia University, New York, NY

I LIKE to pray before I go to bed every night. I have a novena that I say while stretching. I also read the daily meditations out of a monthly book called *Word Among Us*. This allows me to have some type of meditation from the Bible and often relates to what I am feeling in my relationship with Christ. Lastly, I like to thank God for the wonderful things and people that he places in my life. I feel that if I can think of at least one thing during that day that caused me joy, it was a great day. These little brief things help keep me focused and close to God.

Sharon L.
Freshman, Business Management
Rocky Mountain College, Billings, MT

For Further Reflection

- **Randomly choose a Scripture verse. What does it say to me about God or my life?**

- **What are some music lyrics that are especially meaningful to me? Why?**

- **Write a definite plan for beginning a journaling program.**

- **What is my preferred time of day for spiritual reading, writing, and reflection?**

Dawn and Dusk

Prayer in my opinion is nothing else than an intimate sharing between friends; it means taking time frequently to be alone with him who we know loves us.

—Saint Teresa of Avila[7]

The quiet of dawn and our morning rising set the tone for the day. We all know what happens when we awake rushed and weary after mindlessly tumbling into sleep the previous night. And we know the difference that a calm, spacious greeting of the morning can make. Ending our day well is equally important and prepares our body for restorative rest and anticipation for a new day. At dusk, with the setting sun, or at bedtime, we have the opportunity to reflect upon the triumphs and failures of the day, and release what no longer contains life-giving potential for ourselves or others. Dusk and dawn are the ideal time to intimately share the details of our everyday life with our Lord, Jesus Christ, who is our constant companion through all hours.

EVERY morning I like to pray in the shower. It's guaranteed, uninterrupted time that I have with Jesus. I offer my day to God and ask him to be with me and shine through me in all that I do that day.

Christine M.
Freshman, Journalism and History
Saint Ambrose University, Davenport, IA

SINCE being at college, finding time for prayer has been really difficult. In September I learned that our dorm chapel was open all the time. So every morning I wake up and go sit in the back pew. As I am waking up, I talk to God, telling him my gratitude for living another day and praying for the wonderful people who have touched my life. Sometimes when the weather is warm, I walk out toward the woods. There is something about trees and leaves and the singing birds that just fills my heart with God's presence. If it is cold out, I love to sit in our dorm's parlor and just watch the people walking by and the snow outside while praying and reflecting on life.

Rachel S.
Freshman, Music Education
Saint Mary's College, Notre Dame, IN

SINCE I was in kindergarten, my parents would wake us up every morning at 5:30 to pray together. At the time I hated this, but when I went to college and stopped this routine I realized I really needed to start my day with prayer; just not that early! So now I do my own version of my family's morning prayer. I use my breviary to read the daily Scriptures. Then I use the *Living Faith* booklet to read the reflection on the readings.

Angela S.
Senior, Liberal Studies
Central Missouri State University,
Warrensburg, MO

I'VE made it a habit to acknowledge God the moment I realize I am awake in the morning—sometimes even before completely opening my eyes. This sets the mood for the whole day and helps me prepare for whatever comes my way for the next twenty-four hours. I also say a prayer of thanksgiving at the end of the day, and ask God that I may have "a restful sleep and a peaceful death." I have a votive candle that I light when I read, study, write papers, and do homework. It reminds me of God's presence and blessings, which allow me at that moment to be alive. It is my way of praising God while I work.

Joseph S.
Senior, Theology
Saint Ambrose University, Davenport, IA

EVERY night, as I lay in bed, I thank God for another day. In the morning, as I shower, I reflect on what aspect of my life I will try to improve that day. I am working on acknowledging everyone I pass, instead of that awkward glance away that most of us do. In acknowledging everyone, we acknowledge God and his presence in them. Who knows, a smile just might change someone's day.

Robert J.
Freshman, Mechanical Engineering
Purdue University, West Lafayette, IN

WHEN praying at night, I
tend to start out with a little breathing exercise while mentally thinking about Saint Margaret of Scotland (my confirmation saint) and God. In the mornings, I like to stand at my dorm window and pray before leaving the room.

Elisa B.
Junior, History
Merrimack College, North Andover, MA

SOME nights I fall asleep to religious music. My favorites are "O Holy Night" and "Ave Maria" sung by Pavarotti. The music takes me into a profound spiritual state. I fall asleep with images of those I love and the prayers that are deepest in my heart.

Lauren P.
Graduate Program, Social Work
Columbia University, New York, NY

I FIND that a lot of times I get caught up in my day, but at nighttime when I lay down for bed, I always take time to pray. I use a little prayer I've said since I was a little girl, and then another prayer that an old youth minister used. It's: "God first, others second, you last." Always start with thanking God for things he's done, and then pray for others, and lastly your-self. It's kind of neat.

Karen W.
Senior, Business
Colorado State University, Fort Collins, CO

I ALWAYS pray at night before I go to sleep. It's one of the few quiet times I have to myself and prayer prevents me from going to sleep worried, angry, or upset. To set the mood I'll make the Sign of the Cross and release any pressing emotion I may have at that time. Then I listen and let the Spirit move me to what I need to do. Sometimes I request guidance, comfort, or forgiveness; other times I pray in thanksgiving for a blessing or an act of grace. If I have nothing to say, I'll start reciting traditional prayers like the Our Father or Hail Mary to keep the communication flowing. When I feel that both sides have said all they need to and the moment is over, I'll end with another Sign of the Cross and roll over, knowing that in the morning I'll have the power to do better.

Julia S.
Senior, English
Central Missouri State University,
Warrensburg, MO

I HAVE always tried to pray

before falling asleep each night, but since coming to college I find that my body often has other plans and I fall asleep soon after my head hits the pillow. In a desperate struggle to try to keep prayer active in my life, I looked outside my own concepts of prayer. I now pray as I walk to class each morning. I also have learned that actions are a form of prayer as well. I have returned to volunteering and trying to keep active in the community at large.

Brian T.
Junior, Industrial and Operations
Engineering and Pre-Medicine
University of Michigan, Ann Arbor, MI

I PRAY in these words before I

go to bed: "Thank you, dear God, for giving me another day to live. Thank you for the air and the light. Thank you for having me here and giving me the opportunity to study. Please take care of my parents and siblings. Bless all of our projects and guide us with your light. Amen."

Teti G.
Freshman, Aerospace Engineering
University of Arizona, Tucson, AZ

For Further Reflection

- When are specific times, during the day or night, when I especially feel God's presence?

- What are my mornings like? How can I make them a time for prayer?

- Describe a prayer I say before going to bed at night.

- Which part of the day do I find most fruitful for prayer?

Notes

1. Henri J.M. Nouwen, *With Open Hands* (Notre Dame, IN: Ave Maria Press, 1995).
2. Saint Francis de Sales, *Thy Will Be Done: Letters to Persons in the World*, Extensive editorial revisions and improvements in the translation originally published in The Library of Saint Frances de Sales, vol. 1, Letters to Persons in the World, translated by the Very Reverend Henry Benedict Mackey London: Burns & Oats, Ltd.; New York, Cincinnati, Chicago: Benziger Brothers, 1894. (Manchester, NH: Sophia Institute Press, 1995), p. 27.
3. Meister Eckhart, source unknown.
4. Saint Thérèse of Lisieux, *The Autobiography of Saint Thérèse of Lisieux: The Story of a Soul*, Translated by John Beevers (Garden City, NY: Image Books, 1957), p. 66.
5. John O'Donohue, *Eternal Echoes* (New York, NY: Cliff Street Books, 1999), p. 52.
6. Inscribed on a fountain in The Harry and Jeanette Weinberg Center, home to the renowned Center for Women's Health and Medicine in Baltimore, Maryland. The inscription is attributed to the founder of the Sisters of Mercy, Mother Catherine McAuley.

7. Saint Teresa of Avila, *The Collected Works of Saint Teresa of Avila*, vol. 1, 2nd ed., rev. Translated by Kieran Kavanaugh, O.C.D. and Otilio Rodriguez, O.C.D. (Washington D.C.: ICS Publications, 1985), p. 96.

Pegge Bernecker is a spiritual director and retreat leader from Fort Collins, Colorado. A former campus minister at Colorado State University, she is on the faculty for the Center for Spirituality at Work in Denver.

CPSIA information can be obtained
at www.ICGtesting.com
Printed in the USA
FFOW05n2013280514